Sugar Ray Leonard

By
Carolyn Gloeckner

Edited By
Dr. Howard Schroeder
Professor in Reading and Language Arts
Dept. of Elementary Education
Mankato State University

Produced & Designed By

Baker Street Productions, Ltd.

CRESTWOOD HOUSE
Mankato, Minnesota
U.S.A.

LIBRARY OF CONGRESS CATALOGING IN PUBLICATION DATA

Gloeckner, Carolyn.
  Sugar Ray Leonard.

  SUMMARY: A biography of the welter weight champion who lost only one out of the thirty-three matches of his career.
  1. Leonard, Sugar Ray, 1956-   —Juvenile literature. 2. Boxers (Sports)—United States—Biography—Juvenile literature. [1. Leonard, Sugar Ray, 1956-   . 2. Boxers (Sports) 3. Afro-Americans—Biography] I. Schroeder, Howard. II. Title.
  GV1132.L42G58   1985   796.8'3'0924   [B]   [92]   84-9610
  ISBN 0-89686-253-4

International Standard Book Number:	Library of Congress Catalog Card Number:
0-89686-253-4	84-9610

PHOTO CREDITS

Cover: Focus on Sports
Wide World Photos: 4-5, 8, 16, 21, 23, 24-25, 28, 31, 34-35, 40, 46-67
Baltimore Sun: 7, 11, 15, 18, 39
Focus on Sports: 26, 32, 33
United Press: 36, 43
Sports Illustrated: (Manny Millam) 44, 45

Hwy. 66 South, Box 3427
Mankato, MN 56002-3427

TABLE OF CONTENTS

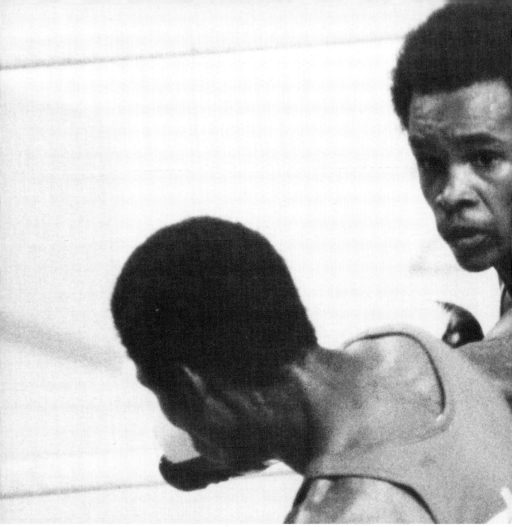

Sugar Ray fights Andres Aldama for the gold medal at the Montreal Olympics.

THE GOLD MEDAL WINNER

Sugar Ray Leonard was tired. He had fought and won six matches in the last two weeks. He had beaten the best

amateur boxers from Cuba, Poland, East Germany, Britain, the Soviet Union, and Sweden.

It was the night of July 31, 1976, at the Montreal Olympics. Leonard had just battled it out with Cuba's Andres Aldama for the Olympic gold medal in the 139-pound class. He had won—easily. Now he held the gold. The stadium was filled with cheering fans. But nobody could find Sugar Ray Leonard. Sugar Ray had disappeared.

His parents and friends searched for him. Finally, his coach, Dave Jacobs, asked Leonard's parents where their camper was parked. They had driven up from Maryland to see their son fight. Sure enough, when Jacobs reached the camper, Sugar Ray was inside. He was dressed in his boxing trunks. He was still wearing his gold medal. He told Jacobs that he was ready to go home.

Jacobs argued with him. It was a fourteen-hour drive back to Maryland. Sugar Ray said he had a plane ticket. Jacobs suggested he get a good night's sleep, and then fly home the next day. "No," said Sugar Ray, "I want to go home right now." He didn't even want to go back to the Olympic Village to pick up his clothes.

HOME AGAIN

So Sugar Ray, his parents, and Jacobs headed home that night in the camper. As they drove, Sugar Ray talked about his plans. He wanted to go to college. He wanted to do something that involved kids. His boxing career was behind him now.

When they reached the border of the United States, the border guard took a second look at Sugar Ray. From watching the Olympics on TV he recognized the young boxer right away. Sugar Ray's smile and good looks had charmed the television audiences.

Sugar Ray took time to visit students at a Baltimore school.

"Is this really Sugar Ray Leonard's camper?" he asked. Sugar Ray leaned out the door and showed him the gold medal. "Can I touch it?" asked the guard.

That was just a taste of what was to come. A police honor guard met the camper at the Maryland border and escorted them home. Thousands of Sugar Ray's neighbors came out to cheer his arrival.

Back home, Sugar Ray was swept up in a lot of activity. He was asked to speak to youth groups. Strangers invited him to parties. Others had ideas to make money from his sudden fame. His parents' house was always full of people.

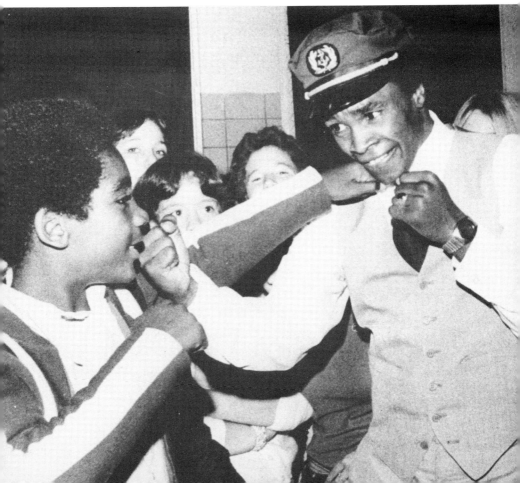

FADING FAME

The months passed, and things were not going as Sugar Ray had hoped. He had won an Olympic gold medal, but that was all. Nobody came up with an idea that would help him make money from his newfound fame. He was not hired to do commercials. He had to face it—he was plain old Ray Leonard again. There was no money for college. He couldn't even support his son, Ray Jr., and Ray Jr.'s mother, Juanita.

Things went from bad to worse. His mother, Gertha, had two mild heart attacks. His father was found to have a serious health condition called meningitis. He had two

parents in the hospital and the bills were piling up. There was no money to pay them.

In a few months everything had changed. He had gone from being Olympic gold-medal winner Sugar Ray to being Ray Leonard, a kid from a poor neighborhood who had done some boxing.

RAY'S EARLY YEARS

It seemed to Sugar Ray that he had been poor forever. Born on May 17, 1956, in North Carolina, he was the fifth of seven children. His parents, Gertha and Cicero, had to work hard to keep food on the table. There were so many mouths to feed! Gertha named her new baby son Ray Charles, after the blind singer. She was pleased when Ray turned out to have a good singing voice. He often sang with his sisters in church.

When young Ray was four years old, the family moved. First they moved to Washington, D.C. Then they moved to Seat Pleasant in the Maryland suburbs. Finally, they settled in Palmer Park, another suburb in Maryland. Palmer Park was mostly black, and often the people were poor.

Gertha remembers that Ray was shy and quiet. He was never any trouble at school. Ray liked to play with his dog. He read a lot—mainly comic books.

Ray remembers something else. He remembers that there never seemed to be enough money. His mother

Sugar Ray's professional career was going nowhere.

9

worked as a nurse and his father worked nights at a grocery store to keep the family going. But they couldn't afford any extras. When Ray's class went on a field trip, there wasn't the money for Ray to go. So on field-trip days, Ray stayed home. He wore his brothers' hand-me-down clothing. Even lunch money was a problem at times.

THE MAKING OF
A CHAMPION

When Ray was fourteen, his older brother Roger turned him on to boxing. Roger had been going to the Palmer Park Recreation Center to box. The Center's director, Ollie Dunlap, had formed a boxing team and spent $45 for two pairs of boxing gloves. At the Center, Ray got to know the volunteer coaches. One was Janks Morton, an insurance salesman. The other was Dave Jacobs, a delivery-truck driver. Both men were to become friends and later played an important part in Ray's life.

Jacobs says that Ray was a good kid. "Very shy, but he worked very hard. He came to the gym and did everything you told him to do."

"I wanted it so badly," Ray remembers. "I had to keep going."

Keep going he did! He had a natural grace and quickness, but he wasn't built like a boxer. Ray was slim and sleek. He took to boxing as if he were born to it. He was

*Dave Jacobs tapes Sugar Ray's hands before
a workout.*

smart, too. He learned easily, remembering and using what Jacobs and Morton told him.

In 1973, Ray won the National Golden Gloves championship in the 132-pound class. That year was special for another reason, too. On November 22, Ray and Juanita Wilkinson had a baby son. They named the child Ray Charles Jr. The next year, Ray was a national American Athletic Union junior boxing champion. A year after that he was a Pan-American winner. During these years, he was training under poor conditions. The Recreation Center did not even have a ring until 1976. Ray trained in the middle of the gym, on the floor. When the basketball team came for practice, he had to go.

It takes money to travel to matches, and Ray's family had little to spare. So, to pay Ray's expenses, neighbors and friends gave what they could. Food sales, run by Jacobs' wife, paid for some of the trips. During the week she cooked chicken, ribs, and ham hocks. On Saturday and Sunday she sold them.

A DREAM FULFILLED

For Ray and his trainers, the Olympic games were to be the peak of his career. He trained hard. First he spent a month in Burlington, Vermont, at the Olympic training camp. Then he spent another month at the Olympic Village in Montreal. It was hard being away from his family and friends.

There had been trouble at other Olympic games. There was a fear that terrorists would try to hurt the Olympic athletes. So the Montreal Olympic Village was guarded night and day. A high fence was built around it. Ray didn't like the feeling that he might be in danger. He didn't like being so far from home. But he worked hard. When the games started, he was ready. He had hurt his hands weeks before, though, and they wouldn't heal. He tried soaking them and rubbing in creams and ointments, but still there was pain. He had to nurse them along to keep fighting.

Ray's 150th amateur fight was the fight for the gold medal. He was exhausted, but thrilled when he won. He said, "I have fulfilled my dream. This is the end of the journey."

American fans went wild for this talented boxer. He was so nice, so good-looking, so well-spoken. At the Olympics, people took to calling him Sugar Ray, after Sugar Ray Robinson, a famous professional boxer.

A famous professional boxer was just what he didn't want to be. After the Olympics, he was ready to quit boxing forever. He had other plans.

AN IMPORTANT DECISION

With both parents in the hospital, Sugar Ray felt he had to do something. His family was the most important thing in his life. He spent a week in Burlington, Vermont, thinking about the future. He had made some friends there during his Olympic training. He talked to them and thought a lot about what to do next.

When Sugar Ray got home, he went to Jacobs and Morton. Morton took him to a friend, a lawyer named Mike Trainer. Trainer offered to help Sugar Ray get started as a professional fighter. He would act as the boxer's lawyer and unpaid secretary.

Trainer asked Morton if Sugar Ray might make $20,000 in a year.

"A hundred thousand," Morton said firmly. "Before his career is over, he'll be the biggest thing in boxing." At the time, neither man could have dreamed of the millions that Leonard would make as a boxer.

GETTING STARTED AS A BOXER

Trainer got busy. First of all, they needed money. They had to support Sugar Ray's training until he could get his

Sugar Ray heads to the gym.

first paying match. So Trainer collected $21,000 from people who wanted to help. It was to be a loan. Sugar Ray would pay it back, at eight percent interest, within four years.

Dave Jacobs became Sugar Ray's trainer. For a manager, they chose Angelo Dundee, who had handled Muhammed Ali's boxing career. They couldn't have chosen better. Dundee had been in the business since 1948. He believed in bringing a fighter along slowly. "Slow

15

Sugar Ray in 1977.

teach," he called it. He planned to arrange matches with fighters that Sugar Ray might have a chance to beat. Dundee spoke Spanish, so he was able to talk to managers of Latin American fighters. Most importantly, his style matched Sugar Ray's. Both were considerate of others. "It costs nothing to be nice," Dundee said.

SUGAR RAY'S FIRST MATCH

For Sugar Ray's first professional match, Dundee chose to pit him against Luis "The Bull" Vega. Sugar Ray was to get $20,000. He was also to get the first $5,000 after ticket sales reached $30,000, and half of all ticket sales over $35,000. The match was set for February 5, 1977. It was to be held in Baltimore, Maryland. The city was close to Sugar Ray's home. The hope was that a lot of people would come to see the "hometown boy." That would boost ticket sales.

Vega would be a tough opponent. He had never been knocked down. For the match, Vega was being paid only $650. But he knew that if he won, he would have a chance at bigger fights.

When Sugar Ray entered the ring, he was smiling. At first, the boxers seemed to be testing each other. Each wanted to learn the other's weaknesses and fighting style. But in the second round, Sugar Ray changed styles.

Suddenly, he was punching and jabbing quickly and confidently. It had been a long time since his Olympic gold-medal fight. Some of the sharpness had worn off. But he seemed to know what he was doing. In round five, Leonard slowed a little, but by round six he was back punching and jabbing. After the sixth and final round, the judges declared the match a "shutout." Sugar Ray had won every round.

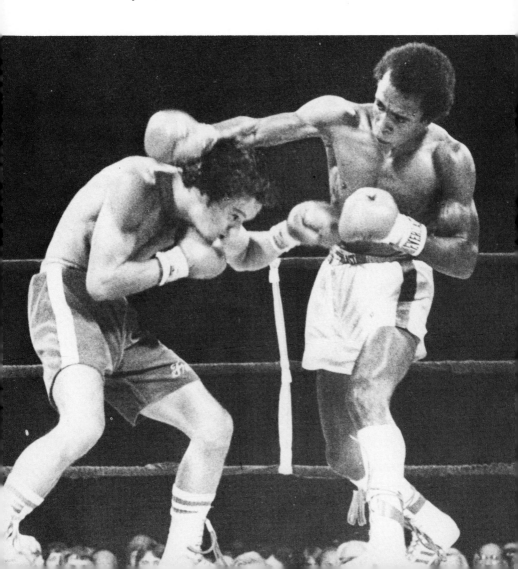

Leonard was impressed by Vega's spirit and skill. He said, "I hit him so many combinations and he still didn't go down. He was still there in the end. Vega is a champion, too."

Sugar Ray's total earnings from the fight came to a little over $40,000. It was enough. Leonard paid off the $21,000 loan. Then he paid his parents' hospital bills.

Did Sugar Ray regret having chosen to become a professional boxer? "It wasn't an easy decision," he said, "I meant it when I said at the Olympics that I didn't want to fight anymore. But I felt I owed it to my family. They are down and I am capable of lifting them up and putting them in a good financial position."

THE TITLE FIGHT

There were more fights. Sugar Ray trained hard for each one and always won. Leonard was a "smart fighter." He wanted to find out how each of his opponents fought. Then he would figure out the best way to beat them. He spent hour after hour watching taped fights. He also spent many hours in the ring, practicing punches, jabs, and footwork. He spent hours running, too.

CHOOSING AN OPPONENT

Sugar Ray was ready for a title match. The two World Boxing Council (WBC) champions in the welterweight

After beating Vega, Sugar Ray knocked out Frank Santore.

(147-pound) class were Jose Cuevos and Wilfredo Benitez. Cuevos was known for his damaging punches. More than one of his opponents had gone to the hospital. Benitez seemed like a better choice. He was twenty-one, and he was outgrowing the welterweight class.

Dundee and Benitez's manager had long arguments about the fight. Where and when should it be held? Which fighter would get most of the earnings? Finally, it was decided to hold the fight in Las Vegas, Nevada. There would be a lot of money for the fighters! ABC offered $1.9 million to televise the fight. There would be another $500,000 from Caesars Palace, where the fight would take place. Sugar Ray would get $1 million and Benitez would get $1.2 million. There was a lot at stake for both of them.

BENITEZ VS. LEONARD

The fight was exciting. Right away, Leonard tried a jab, a righthand punch, and a hook—a combination that connected. Benitez danced away, though, and it wasn't until the third round that Sugar Ray moved in again. This time Sugar Ray got Benitez with a left jab. Benitez went down, but quickly got to his feet.

In the fourth round, Benitez changed tactics. Suddenly, Benitez and Leonard were like twins. Benitez was fighting Sugar Ray style! Benitez easily turned aside Leonard's overhand right punches. Sugar Ray was confused. Before now, it had been easy to connect with a punch. Now it was

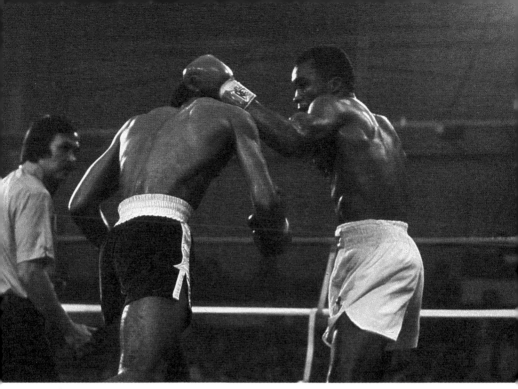

*In a hard match, Sugar Ray beat Benitez to
become champion!*

like fighting with his reflection in a mirror. Dundee told
Sugar Ray to "go downstairs" and try some body
punches. But Sugar Ray complained that Benitez seemed
to disappear when the punches started coming.

In the sixth round, the fighters cracked foreheads.
Sugar Ray wasn't badly hurt, but the Champion suffered a
gash. The blood flowed down his face, almost blinding
him. Benitez had another problem, too. He had hurt his
left thumb early in the match. But he wouldn't quit. Sugar
Ray punched and managed to land some blows. But
Benitez took them, unhurt. In the eleventh round,
Leonard landed a punch that knocked the champion's

mouthpiece loose. But Benitez fought on. In the final round, the fifteenth, both fighters "went to town." Both felt that the match had been a tie so far, so both fought hard.

Sugar Ray caught Benitez on the chin. Down went Benitez, dazed. Although he got up and tried for more, the referee stopped the fight after two more punches. Benitez had lost—his first loss in thirty-eight fights. Sugar Ray Leonard was still unbeaten after twenty-six professional matches. And now Sugar Ray was the new WBC welterweight champion.

THE CHAMPION!

Sugar Ray was full of admiration for his opponent. "No one can make me miss punches like he did," Sugar Ray said. "I kept thinking, 'Man, this guy's really good'!"

Benitez was impressed with Leonard, too. "He won easy. He's a great challenger. He became champion beating me. I want to wish him good luck, and God bless him."

Sugar Ray had taken quite a beating during the fight. This was the part that he hated. The bruises, the swelling, the aches. He was to be a guest on *The Merv Griffin Show* at Caesars Palace that night. The makeup man had to work hard on his face to make him look good enough to go on TV. Juanita and little Ray were shocked by his ap-

Sugar Ray and Roberto have some fun before their fight.

pearance, too. Sugar Ray knew it was part of the game—and once again wished that he were not fighting for a living. He still wanted to retire from boxing. He also wanted to get out of boxing before he got badly hurt. But he needed to earn enough money to take care of his family.

CHALLENGE, DEFEAT, AND VICTORY

When Sugar Ray fought Roberto Duran in June, 1980, he was on top of the world. He was the defending champion. And he was fighting in Montreal, where, four years before, he had won an Olympic gold medal. It seemed to everyone that nothing could possibly go wrong. He had fought and won twenty-seven professional bouts.

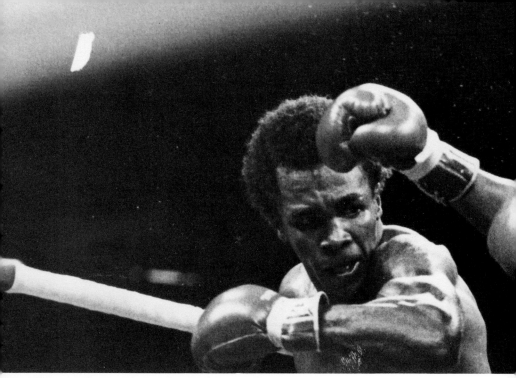

Duran misses with a right during the Montreal fight.

SLEEPWALKING

But something happened just before the Duran fight was to start. Leonard blanked out. He said later that he fell into a kind of trance. He felt as if he were sleepwalking. His opponent, however, had no such problem. Roberto Duran was feeling as strong as a tiger, and as brave. In seventy-one fights, he had lost only one.

"When I get into the ring to fight, I always give my best,"said Duran. That June night in Montreal was no exception.

The crowd loved the fight. It seemed as if both men were giving their all. They brawled back and forth all over

the ring. Each man ducked and danced, trying to lure the other closer. Both landed fierce punches. But Duran was clearly the stronger fighter. By the third round, Juanita, Ray's wife, was crying. She couldn't bear to watch Sugar Ray being hurt so badly.

Duran pounded Sugar Ray without let up. He drove the Champion against the ropes, punching as he went. Sugar Ray tried to keep away from Duran's punches. Leonard's speed in the ring didn't matter any more. Duran didn't wait for Sugar Ray to take the lead—he went after Sugar Ray with all he had. Leonard couldn't get in his famous jab.

A MATTER OF TACTICS

Later, both men's trainers described their fighters' tactics. Duran had been told to go after Sugar Ray. He was not to give the champion a chance to get close to him. Above all, he was to use his strength to keep Sugar Ray on the run. Dundee had told Leonard to "fight smart." After all, Duran was clearly the stronger fighter. To win, Sugar Ray would have to keep away from Duran and punch when he could. Instead, Sugar Ray played Duran's game. Dundee said, "He tried to outstrong the guy. Duran was being Duran, and Leonard was going with him. The guy who had more practice won the fight. It was all Duran."

At the end of fifteen rounds, the judges' decision came as no surprise. Roberto Duran was now the new welterweight champion.

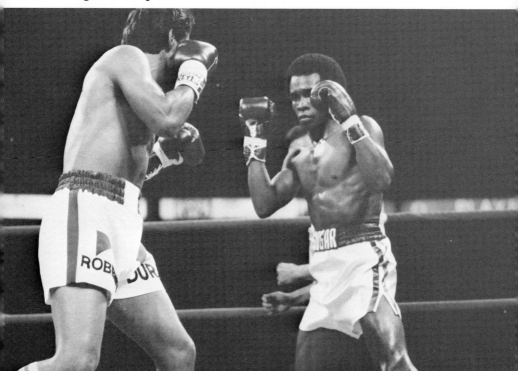

CHAMPION NO MORE

Sugar Ray, bruised and exhausted, would receive more than $8 million for the fight. It had been the richest prizefight in boxing history. But he was discouraged. For his part, Mike Trainer was satisfied that Sugar Ray had given enough to boxing. "I don't enjoy seeing him get hit," Trainer said. "As far as I am concerned, he can pack it in." Leonard was a rich man now. He didn't really need boxing anymore.

Sugar Ray and Juanita went on a vacation to Hawaii to rest and discuss their future. After a few days, the boxer began to feel much better. Talk of retirement stopped. After a jog on the beach one day, Sugar Ray told his wife about his plans. He had to fight Duran again. This time he would win.

Sugar Ray felt he had learned a lot from the Duran fight. He found he could take a punch with the best of them. He hadn't fallen—he had even landed a few solid punches of his own. He said he had gained five years of boxing experience in that one night in Montreal. He had fought Duran, Duran's way. But his next match with Duran would bring back his quick footwork, his jab. He would play some angles. He would fight Duran his own way.

Sugar Ray tried to keep away from Duran's punches.

DURAN AGAIN!

He began training harder than he had ever trained before. Angelo Dundee showed him how to keep changing angles as he fought. He learned how to go at his opponent from a different direction every time. There were plenty of people who said this wouldn't be enough. They claimed that Sugar Ray had to fight like Duran. If he tried anything else, he would be knocked out.

But the night of November 25, 1980, Sugar Ray showed that he could do it. He went after Duran just the way he said he would. He stayed away from the flurry of punches

and jabs. He danced on the balls of his feet and bashed away at his opponent. By the seventh round, it was obvious that Duran was no match for Leonard. And in the eighth, Duran ran out of steam. He turned away when Sugar Ray came for him. The referee shouted, "fight!" But Duran would not. *"No mas,"* he said. "No more." Leonard was declared the winner. He had recaptured his title.

LEONARD VS. HEARNS— THE TITLE DEFENDED

The year 1981, was one of the best for Sugar Ray. He couldn't be beaten. The gate receipts piled up into a small fortune. Sugar Ray appeared as a guest and commentator on many TV shows.

Then came the richest fight of Sugar Ray's career. He was to fight World Boxing Association (WBA) welterweight champion Thomas Hearns. For the fight, Hearns would get $5.1 million. Sugar Ray's share was to be a whopping $11 million.

PLANNING AND TACTICS

Sugar Ray really wanted to win. He sized up his opponent carefully. Thomas Hearns was a big man—over six

In the second Duran fight, Sugar Ray showed what he could do!

feet tall. He was really too big for a welterweight. To keep his weight under the 147-pound mark, Hearns had to work hard. He would have to take off pounds in the form of water. That meant sitting and sweating in a sauna for hours. However, Hearns was a tough, strong fighter and a hard puncher. Leonard would have to be ready for him if he had any hope of winning.

THE CHAMPIONSHIP FIGHT

The night of the fight it was hot in Las Vegas. The Caesars Palace ring was bathed in floodlights for the TV cameras. Everything was on Sugar Ray's side. Already dried out, Hearns would soon tire in the heat. Angelo Dundee told Sugar Ray to keep Hearns moving and missing, to tire him out.

Sugar Ray did his best. But in the first round, Hearns didn't seem to want to get going. Both fighters danced around the ring, as if they had all the time in the world. In the second round, Hearns connected with a punch to Leonard's head. But Sugar Ray had learned long before how to handle punches. When he could, he pulled his head back as the punch landed. It was a trick he had learned from Ken Norton and Muhammed Ali. To fans, it looked as if the punch had connected. But it had only touched Leonard. He wasn't hurt at all. Sugar Ray missed Hearns with a punch to the head, then hit him hard to the body.

Sugar Ray had learned how to take a punch.

Hearns came back, hitting Sugar Ray's face, especially his left eye. A few weeks before, Leonard had caught a punch there while training. Now the eye began to swell. That meant that the boxer couldn't see quite as well. Hearns aimed punch after punch at that eye during the match.

The third round brought a change in Sugar Ray. He went after Hearns with powerful jabs—first a left, then a right. As the round ended, Sugar Ray was raining punches on his opponent. Hearns didn't seem to know what to do.

Dundee warned him after the round to move more. "Don't stand there and fight him. Move. Make him move!"

Leonard did just that. During the fourth and fifth rounds he moved all around Hearns. During the sixth, Hearns made a fatal error. He tried a right, giving Sugar Ray the opening he was looking for. Sugar Ray hooked Hearns in the ribs with a hard blow. It was a punishing

Hearns took a solid punch to the ribs.

punch, one from which Hearns never came back during the rest of the fight.

From the seventh round on, Hearns tried to protect his

ribs and stay away from Leonard. It proved impossible.
Sugar Ray danced after him and connected with rights,
hooks, and combination punches.

By the ninth round, though, Leonard had his own wor-
ries. His left eye was giving him trouble. He had only

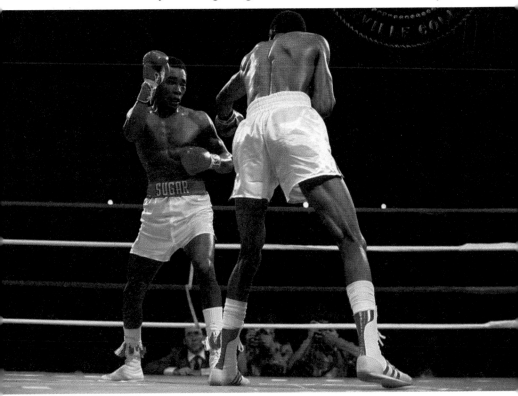

*By the ninth round, Sugar Ray had lost
fifty percent of his eyesight.*

about fifty percent of the vision left. He was starting to be
careful—too careful. Hearns regained some confidence,
and by the eleventh round Hearns was mixing it up again.

In the fourteenth round, Sugar Ray knocked
Hearns into the ropes.

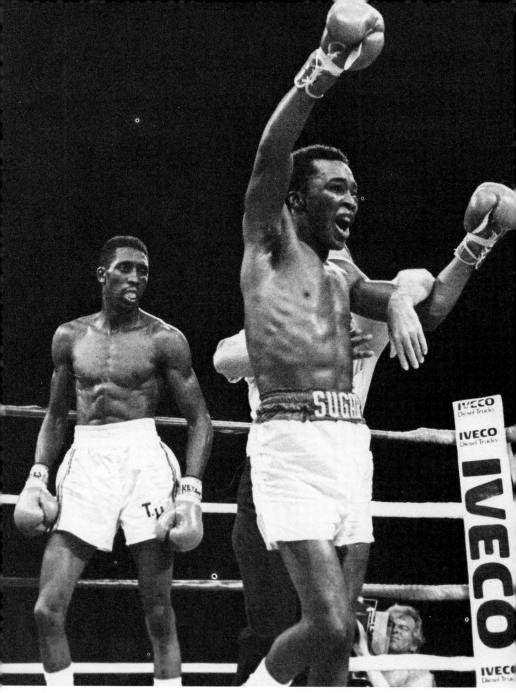

The referee stopped the fight, and Sugar Ray yelled for joy!

He punched away at Leonard's eye. Sugar Ray was stunned by the blows, but he was not giving in. The thirteenth round proved to be Hearns's undoing. Leonard caught him with a right, then hit him with a flurry of twenty-five punches. Hearns fell back into the ropes.

In the fourteenth round, Hearns seemed to have no strength left. The referee watched as Sugar Ray punched Hearns again and again. Finally, he stopped the match. Sugar Ray Leonard had won! He was the holder of both the WBC and the WBA welterweight championships!

But for his son, who had watched the fight from ringside, the win was not so important. Little Ray looked at his father's swollen and bruised face. "Daddy, why do you keep on fighting?" Ray Jr. asked. Sugar Ray Leonard must have wondered, too. He was exhausted. Worst of all, he could barely see out of his left eye.

A FALLING SHADOW

On April 22, 1982, Sugar Ray was jogging around an indoor track, training for a big fight. He was to defend his welterweight title against Roger Stafford. As he ran, he was annoyed by a floating spot in his left eye. He insisted on seeing a doctor. The doctor gave him eyedrops, which didn't help. So he went to another doctor. This one took a look and said that part of Leonard's retina—the membrane at the back of the eye—had been shaken loose. It was wrinkled and floating, and that part of Sugar Ray's eye would not work properly. The thing to do was to operate to put the retina back in place.

HOME TO MARYLAND

Sugar Ray did what he always had done in a crisis. He went home to Maryland. Leonard, Juanita, Mike Trainer, Janks Morton, and Sugar Ray's father met at Johns Hopkins Hospital in Maryland. The little group was sad and quiet as eye specialist, Dr. Ronald Michels, agreed with the diagnosis. Leonard had a detached retina. It was a condition that was more common among older people. In the young, it was usually caused by a blow to the head. If it weren't treated, Sugar Ray could go blind. Proper treatment meant an operation to "paste" the retina back into place. Even so, success was not guaranteed. Leonard could still lose the vision in that eye.

Juanita began to sob. She had hoped that the injury wasn't serious. Sugar Ray tried to comfort her. "Don't cry," he said. "Everything's going to be all right."

Dr. Michels knew how important the diagnosis was to the fighter. It could mean that he would never box again. "We have a little time," the doctor said. "You don't have to decide right now. Go and get another opinion, if you want."

Trainer asked if they could go somewhere and discuss it. They went into another room. Trainer said to Sugar Ray,

Howard Cosell announces Sugar Ray's retirement.

"OK, pal, you got it. Now, let's solve it and get on with it!"

"Let's do it," the boxer said.

THE OPERATION

In a short operation, doctors repaired the damaged retina. But they warned Sugar Ray against fighting, for at least six months. He needed time to heal. Sugar Ray was glad to take the time off. He felt that this might be a sign. Perhaps it was time for him to quit.

He would wait six months. Then he would decide whether he would continue his boxing career. The November following the operation, Sugar Ray made an announcement. He was retiring from boxing. He would never fight again.

Sugar Ray's family joined him when his retirement was announced.

But the ring drew him like a magnet. He waited a year. Then, in December, 1983, he made another announcement. He said he was coming back. "Retiring was something I didn't want to do. I was on a roll in my career and then I had to accept stepping down." He said he was only twenty-seven, in his prime. He didn't want to watch the action from the sidelines anymore.

It was more than just that, though. He had watched "Marvelous" Marvin Hagler beat Roberto Duran on TV on November 10. Middleweight Hagler hadn't looked like much of a champion. Leonard decided then and there that he would go back to fighting. And he wouldn't fight only in the welterweight division. He would try the junior middleweight and middleweight divisions, as well. Boxing fans were surprised but pleased. For his first match, Sugar Ray chose to fight Kevin Howard. Howard was ranked No. 14 among welterweights.

MORE PROBLEMS

Sugar Ray's doctor, Edward Ryan, examined him a few weeks before the fight. His left eye had healed perfectly. There was no sign of any trouble. But then he looked at Leonard's right eye. Often, if one retina becomes detached, the other one does, too. Dr. Ryan saw what he had hoped he wouldn't see. The retina in Sugar Ray's right eye was coming loose.

In a five-minute operation, the damage was repaired. Dr. Ryan was glad that they had caught it before the match. If Leonard had fought the match against Howard, he said, "There could have been further damage. We decided right away that he should not fight."

For Sugar Ray, it was a disappointment. At the same time, he knew how lucky he was. After all, he still had his sight. Yet, he wanted so much to fight again—and he wanted most of all to take the championship from "Marvelous" Marvin. What would the coming months bring? No one knew. Fans hoped that Sugar Ray would be able to make his come back. His doctors advised against it. His family and friends were ready to stand behind him, whatever he decided.

On February 24, 1984, Dr. Ryan gave Sugar Ray the go-ahead. His operation had been a success. Leonard could return to the ring. The fight with Kevin Howard was rescheduled for May 11, 1984.

More than a year had passed since his last fight. Everyone wondered if he still had what it took to be a champion. Was he on his way back? Or would he go down to defeat? Fans eagerly waited to find out.

At least one fight fan was not eager to see the match. Harold Weston was not only a fan, he was a fighter. Twice he had tried for the welterweight championship. The second time, fighting Thomas Hearns, he had been injured. Like Sugar Ray, he had a detached retina. The doctors had patched him up.

Weston had wanted a comeback after his eye injury. He

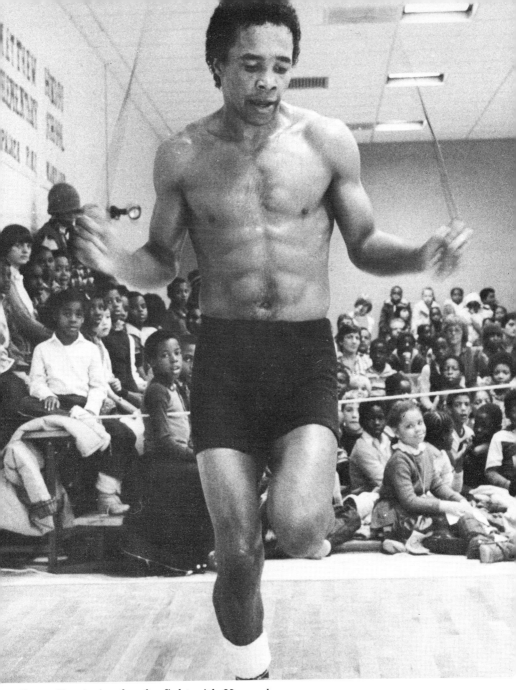

Sugar Ray trains for the fight with Howard.

Sugar Ray missed the excitement of the ring.

had gone to the gym to start training. But something wasn't right. He says now that he knows what that something was. "I was afraid."

Weston never fought again. And he felt that Sugar Ray shouldn't, either. "There's no reason in the world Ray Leonard needs to fight again," said Weston. "He's looking at this the wrong way. He wants to make boxing history, but so what if he wins another title? What's one title piled on top of another title? What good are they if you can't see? What will they mean?"

On the other hand, Ollie Dunlap was thrilled to see Leonard back in the ring. He felt that some of the joy had

Angelo Dundee talks to Sugar Ray during the Howard fight.

gone out of Sugar Ray's life when he retired. "You could tell something was missing. He had the whole world, but what he was missing was that twenty square feet of ring."

It did seem that Sugar Ray had the whole world. He owned a Rolls Royce and a Ferrari. He had just bought a six-bedroom house. He had been a TV commentator at thirty-four fights in 1983. In fact, he had made two million dollars during that year. So why return to the ring?

"I just want to fight again," Sugar Ray said. "I haven't reached my peak. I have a chance for real greatness."

The night of the fight, May 11, 1984, Sugar Ray answered everyone's questions. He was the terrific boxer he'd always been. In the ninth round he hurt Kevin Howard so badly that the fight was stopped. Sugar Ray had won.

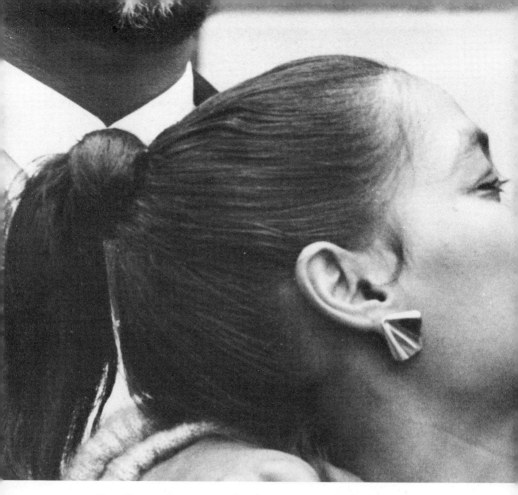

But Sugar Ray surprised everyone. Even though he had won, he decided to quit boxing. Why? Howard had knocked Sugar Ray down in the fourth round. At that moment, Sugar Ray said, "I looked over and saw my wife. I decided I wasn't going to take any more chances and fight anyone else."

So Sugar Ray's boxing career was over. But fans will remember the fighter—and his fights—for many years to come.

Sugar Ray gives Juanita a kiss.

SUGAR RAY LEONARD'S PROFESSIONAL STATISTICS

Dick Eckland, July 18, 1978—won

Floyd Mayweather, September 9, 1978—won

Randy Shields, October 6, 1978—won

Bernardo Prada, November 3, 1978—won

Armando Muniz, December 9, 1978—won

Johnny Gant, January 11, 1979—won

Fernando Marcotte, February 11, 1979—won

Daniel Gonzales, March 24, 1979—won

Adolfo Viruet, April 21, 1979—won

Marcos Geraldo, May 20, 1979—won

Tony Chiaverini, June 24, 1979—won

Pete Ranzany, August 12, 1979—won NABF Welterweight Title

Andy Price, September 28, 1979—won

Wilfred Benitez, November 30, 1979—won WBC Welterweight Title

Dave Green, March 31, 1980—won

Roberto Duran, June 20, 1980—lost WBC Welterweight Title

Roberto Duran, November 25, 1980—won WBC Welterweight Title

Larry Bonds, March 28, 1981—won

Ayub Kalule, June 25, 1981 won

Thomas Hearns, September 16, 1981—won

Bruce Finch, February 15, 1982—won

Kevin Howard, May 11, 1984—won